GENDER EQUITY IN ISLAM

BASIC PRINCIPLES

GENDER EQUITY IN ISLAM

BASIC PRINCIPLES

Jamal Badawi, Ph.D.

American Trust Publications

American Trust Publications, USA

Copyright © 1995 by Jamal Badawi
All rights reserved

First Print 1995
Second Print 1999
Third Print 2003
Fourth Print 2004
Fifth Print 2005

Library of Congress Cataloging in Publication Data
A catalog record for this book is available from the
Library of Congress

ISBN 0-89259-159-5

Printed in Canada.

O you who believe! Stand out firmly for justice, as witnesses to Allah, even as against yourselves, or your parents, or your kin, and whether it be (against) rich or poor: for Allah can best protect both. Follow not the desires (of your hearts), lest you swerve, and if you distort (justice) or decline to do justice, verily Allah is well-acquainted with all that you do. (Qur'an 4:135)

O mankind! Reverence your Guardian-Lord, Who created you from a single person, created, of like nature, his mate, and from them twain scattered (like seeds) countless men and women—fear Allah, through Whom you demand your mutual (rights), and (reverence) the wombs (that bore you): for Allah ever watches over you. (Qur'an 4:1)

The believers, men and women, are protectors, one of another: they enjoin what is just and forbid what is evil: they observe regular prayers, practice regular charity, and obey Allah and His Messenger. On them will Allah pour His Mercy: for Allah is Exalted in power, Wise. (Qur'an 9:71)

Contents

Preface

الحمد لله والصلاة والسلام على رسول الله وعلى آله وصحبه ومن والاه

The issue of gender equity[1] is important, relevant and current. Debates and writings on the subject are increasing and are **diverse** in their perspectives.

The Islamic perspective on the issue is the least understood and most misrepresented by non-Muslims and, at times, by some Muslims as well. The predominant local cultural practices in different parts of the world and the actions of some Muslims tend to reinforce erroneous perceptions of the Islamic perspective. These problems are enhanced by the tendency to treat some juristic **interpretations** as if they were identical with Islam.

As such, there is a pressing need to **reexamine** this issue **in light of the primary sources of Islam.** This brief book is a call for such an overdue task. It is based on a more detailed treatment by the author in album 4 of the Islamic Teachings audiotape series, and may be a prelude to a more comprehensive work on the subject, Allah-willing.

The author wishes to express his gratitude to all reviewers of the manuscript, especially Dr. Ahmad Zaki Hammad, who made several thoughtful comments. Any shortcoming or error is mine, and I seek both forgiveness and correction.

As a reader, your comments, criticisms and suggestions are appreciated and encouraged. Let us all engage in a **collective search for truth,** guided by the revelatory sources of Islam, the Qur'an and Sunnah. Comments may be sent to the author: Jamal Badawi, 8 Laurel Lane, Halifax, NS, B3M 2P6, CANADA.

INTRODUCTION AND METHODOLOGY

ISLAM AND CULTURAL PRACTICES

When writing or speaking about the Islamic position on any issue, one ought to clearly differentiate between the normative teachings of Islam and the **diversity of cultural practices** prevalent among its adherents that may or may not be consistent with those teachings. This paper discusses the normative teachings of Islam with regard to the standing and role of women in society as the criteria by which to judge the practice of Muslims and to evaluate their compliance with Islam.

PRIMARY SOURCES OF ISLAM

In identifying what is "Islamic," it is necessary to make a clear distinction between the **primary sources of Islam**—the Qur'an and the Sunnah of Prophet Muhammad (P)[2]—and the legal opinions derived from them by scholars in regard to specific issues.

FACTORS IN INTERPRETATION

The process of extracting laws from the primary sources is a human function. The surmise of

legal practitioners may therefore vary consider-
ably and be influenced by their specific times, circumstances and cultures. Obviously, opinions and
verdicts of human beings do not enjoy the authority or the finality accorded to the primary sources,
which God revealed. Furthermore, **interpretation**
of the primary sources should consider, among
other things:

1. The **context** of any statement or command-
ment in the Qur'an and the Sunnah
In the case of the Qur'an, this includes both the
context of the surah and the verses under examina-
tion, as well as the general perspective of Islam, its
teachings, and its world-view. As for the *Sunnah*
of the Prophet (P), the same applies to its texts.

2. The **occasion of revelation,** that is, the historical background providing the primary reasons
or causes underlying revelation of a Qur'anic por-
tion or verse to the Prophet (P), which may help to
better elucidate its meaning; and, with regard to
the Sunnah, the event or the incident that occa-
sioned the statement or action of the Prophet

3. The **role of Sunnah** in explaining and defining the meaning of the Qur'anic text
To Muslims, Sunnah is a form of revelation
given to Prophet Muhammad (P), but not verbatim,
as is the case with the Qur'an. As such, authentic
Sunnah is the second primary source of Islamic
teachings, after the Qur'an. It plays the important
roles of defining, explaining and elaborating the

Qur'anic text. For example, the second "pillar" of Islam, prayer, is mentioned in the Qur'an but without details about how it should be performed. Such details were left for Prophet Muhammad (P) to explain based on the instructions of Angel Gabriel.

Disregard or ignorance of Sunnah may lead to **serious errors of interpretation**. At times, the literal or lexical meaning of a term used in the Qur'an may not be its correct meaning if the Prophet (P) qualified or specified what is meant by it. Errors are multiplied when an erroneous literal meaning is **translated** from the original Arabic text of the Qur'an into another language, which, in turn may have its own connotations for the translated words used. A detailed illustration of this type of error is provided in endnote 14.

Following the above methodology, and for the reader's convenience, the issue of gender equity is discussed under four broad headings:

Chapter 1: The Spiritual Aspect
Chapter 2: The Economic Aspect
Chapter 3: The Social Aspect
Chapter 4: The Political and Legal Aspect

It is hoped that, insha'Allah (God-willing), this humble contribution may help in providing a basic frame of reference for more detailed treatments of this vital topic, from an Islamic perspective.

Chapter One

THE SPIRITUAL ASPECT

FOUNDATIONS OF SPIRITUAL AND HUMAN EQUITY

1. According to the Qur'an, men and women have the **same human spiritual nature**.

> 0 mankind! reverence your Guardian-Lord, Who created you from a single person (nafsin-waahidah), created, of like nature, his mate, and from them two scattered (like seeds) countless men and women; reverence Allah through Whom you demand your mutual (rights) and (reverence) the wombs (that bore you): for Allah ever watches over you. . . . (Qur'an 4:1)

> It is He Who created you from a single person and made his mate of like nature, in order that he might dwell with her (in love). When they are united, she bears a light burden and carries it about (unnoticed). When she grows heavy, they both pray to Allah, their Lord (saying) "If You give us a goodly child, we vow we shall (ever) be grateful." (Qur'an 7:189)

> *(He is) the Creator of the heavens and the
> earth: He has made for you pairs from among
> yourselves and pairs among cattle: by this
> means does He multiply you! There is nothing
> whatever like unto Him, and He is the one
> that hears and sees (all things). (Qur'an 42:11)*

2. Both men and women alike are recipients of the "**divine breath**," because they are created with the same human spiritual nature. Indeed, as the Qur'an states, Allah originated them both from a single person or "one soul" (*nafsin-waahidah*). Reflecting the magnitude of this universal divine gift, the Qur'an states:

> *But He fashioned him (the human, or
> insan) in due proportion and breathed into
> him something of His spirit. And He gave
> you (the faculties of) hearing and sight and
> understanding: Little thanks do you give!*[3]
> *(Qur'an 32:9)*

Referring to Adam, the father of both men and women, the Qur'an relates that Allah commanded the angels to bow down (in respect) to him:

> *So if I have fashioned him (in due propor-
> tion) and breathed into him of My spirit, fall
> down in obeisance unto him. (Qur'an 15:29)*

3. Allah has invested both genders with **inherent dignity** and has made men and women, collectively, the trustees of Allah on earth.

We have honored the children of Adam,
provided them with transport on land and
sea, given them for sustenance things good
and pure, and conferred on them special
favors above a great part of Our Creation.
(Qur'an 17:70)

Behold, your Lord said to the angels: "I
will create a vicegerent on earth." They said
"Will you place therein one who will make
mischief therein and shed blood? While we
celebrate Your praises and glorify Your holy
(name)?" He said: "I know what you know
not." (Qur'an 2:30)

4. The Qur'an does not blame woman for the "fall of man," nor does it view pregnancy and childbirth as punishments for "eating from the forbidden tree." On the contrary, the Qur'an depicts Adam and Eve as **equally responsible for their sin in the Garden**, never singling out Eve for blame. It also esteems pregnancy and childbirth as sufficient reasons for the love and respect due to mothers from their children.

0 Adam! You and your wife dwell in the
garden and enjoy (its good things) as you
(both) wish: but approach not this tree or you
(both) run into harm and transgression.
Then Satan began to whisper suggestions
to them, bringing openly before their minds
all their shame that was hidden from them
(before): he said, "Your Lord only forbade

you this tree lest you (both) should become angels or such beings as live forever."

And he swore to them both that he was their sincere adviser. So by deceit he brought about their fall. When they tasted of the tree, their shame became manifest to them and they began to sew together the leaves of the garden over their bodies. And their Lord called unto them: "Did I not forbid you that tree and tell you that Satan was an avowed enemy unto you?"

They said: "Our Lord! we have wronged our own souls: If You forgive us not and bestow not upon us Your mercy, we shall certainly be lost."

(Allah) said: "Get you (both) down with enmity between yourselves. On earth will be your dwelling-place and your means of livelihood for a time." He said: "Therein shall you (both) live and therein shall you (both) die; and from it shall you (both) be taken out (at last). . ."

O you children of Adam! Let not Satan seduce you in the same manner as he got your parents out of the garden, stripping them of their raiment to expose their shame: for he and his tribe watch you from a position where you cannot see them: We made the evil ones friends (only) to those without faith.[4] (Qur'an 7:19-27)

Regarding **pregnancy and childbirth,** the Qur'an states:

> *And We have enjoined on (every) person
> (to be good) to his/her parents: in travail
> upon travail did his/her mother bear him/her
> and in years twain was his/her weaning:
> (hear the command) "Show gratitude to Me
> and to your parents: to Me is (your final)
> Goal." (Qur'an 31:14)*

> *We have enjoined on (every) person kind-
> ness to his/her parents: in pain did his/her
> mother bear him/her and in pain did she give
> him/her birth. The carrying of the (child) to
> his/her weaning is (a period of) thirty months.
> At length, when he/she reaches the age of full
> strength and attains forty years, he/she says
> "0 my Lord! grant that I may be grateful for
> Your favor which You have bestowed upon
> me and upon both my parents and that I may
> work righteousness such as You may approve;
> and be gracious to me in my issue. Truly have
> I turned to You and truly do I bow (to You) in
> Islam (submission)." (Qur'an 46:15)[5]*

5. Men and women have the **same religious
and moral duties and responsibilities.** Each
human being shall face the consequences of his or
her deeds.

> *And their Lord has accepted of them and
> answered them: "Never will I suffer to be lost
> the work of any of you, be he/she male or
> female: you are members one of another. . ."
> (Qur'an 3:195)*

If any do deeds of righteousness, be they male or female, and have faith, they will enter paradise and not the least injustice will be done to them. (Qur'an 4:124)

For Muslim men and women, for believing men and women, for devout men and women, for true men and women, for men and women who are patient and constant, for men and women who humble themselves, for men and women who give in charity, for men and women who fast (and deny themselves), for men and women who guard their chastity, and for men and women who engage much in Allah's praise—for them has Allah prepared forgiveness and great reward. (Qur'an 33:35)

One Day you shall see the believing men and the believing women, how their Light runs forward before them and by their right hands. (Their greeting will be): "Good News for you this Day! Gardens beneath which flow rivers! To dwell therein forever! This is indeed the highest Achievement!" (Qur'an 57:12)

CRITERION FOR "SUPERIORITY"

The Qur'an is quite clear about the issue of the claimed superiority or inferiority of any human, male or female:

> *0 mankind! We created you from a single (pair) of a male and a female, and made you into nations and tribes, that you may know each other. Verily the most honored of you in the sight of Allah is (one who is) the most righteous of you. And Allah has full knowledge and is well acquainted (with all things). (Qur'an 49:13)*

A few observations about this verse may be helpful in tracing the foundation of spiritual and human equality before Allah:

a. It begins by addressing not only Muslims but the whole of mankind, irrespective of their gender and their national or religious backgrounds. As such, it is a universal declaration to all, made by the Creator of all.

b. It states that there is only One Creator of all mankind. As such, there is no room for arguments of superiority based on one's having been created by a "superior" God, as there is only One God (Allah). Nor is there any basis for a caste system based on some having been created in a way which is "different" from others or is superior. As Prophet Muhammad (P) explained, ". . . You all belong to Adam, and Adam was created from dust." In the process of human reproduction, there is no superiority or inferiority; kings and paupers, males and females, are created from what the Qur'an describes as "despised fluid."

Our having been created by the One and Only Creator implies our basic equality before Him; He is just to all.

c. Being a faithful creature, servant and wor-
shipper of the One God is at the heart of one's real
spirituality and humanness. In this, the essence of
gender equality finds its most profound basis.

d. The verse states that all human beings are
created *min thakarin wa-untha,* which can be
translated literally as "of male and female." This
means in pairs, as the Qur'an explicitly mentions
elsewhere (e.g. 78:8). Each component of the pair
is as necessary and as important as the other and
hence is equal to him or her. The wording of this
verse has been commonly translated also as "from
a (single pair of) a male and a female," referring to
Adam and Eve. This serves as a reminder to all
mankind that they belong to the same family, with
one common set of parents. As such they are all
equal, as brothers and sisters in that broad and
"very extended" family.

e. Variations in gender, languages, ethnic
backgrounds and, by implication, religious claims,
do not provide any basis for superiority or inferiority. The implication of "that you may know each
other"(Qur'an 49:13) is that such variations constitute a deliberate mosaic that Allah created, which
is more interesting and more beautiful than a single "color" or a "unisex."

f. Most significant and relevant to the topic at
hand is the clear categorical statement that the
most honored **person** in the sight of Allah is the
one who is most pious and righteous. This precludes any other basis for superiority, including
gender.

6. Nowhere does the Qur'an state that one gender is superior to the other. Some interpreters of the Qur'an mistakenly translate the Arabic word *qiwamah* (responsibility for the family) with the English word "superiority." The Qur'an makes it clear that the **sole basis for the superiority** of any person over another is **piety and righteousness**, not gender, color or nationality.

7. The absence of **women as prophets** or "messengers of Allah" in prophetic history is because of the demands and physical suffering associated with the role of messengers and prophets, and not because of any spiritual inferiority attributed to women.[6] Societies to which prophets, were sent, including the Israelites, pre-Islamic Arabs and others, were largely patriarchal societies. They probably would have been less responsive to the ministry of female messengers of God. In fact, they made things extremely difficult for male messengers.

From this chapter, it is clear that in terms of spirituality and humanness, both genders stand on equal footing before Allah. It is clear also that nowhere in the primary sources of Islam (the Qur'an and Sunnah) do we find any basis for the superiority of one gender over the other. Human misinterpretations or culturally-bound opinions or manipulations are not congruent with what Islam teaches. The full equality of all human beings before Allah is beyond doubt. This equality should not be confused, however, with role differentiation in the spirit of cooperation and complimentarity. This is why equity is a more accurate term than "equality," as explained in endnote 1, and as applied in the remaining chapters of this work.

Chapter Two

THE ECONOMIC ASPECT

THE RIGHT TO POSSESS PERSONAL PROPERTY

One aspect of the world-view of Islam is that **everything in heaven and on earth belongs to Allah**:

> *To Allah belongs all that is in the heavens and on earth. . . (Qur'an 2:284)*

As such, all wealth and resources are ultimately "owned" by Allah. However, out of Allah's Mercy He created mankind to be, collectively, His trustees on earth. In order to help mankind fulfill this trusteeship, He made the universe serviceable to mankind:

> *And He (Allah) has subjected to you, as from Him, all that is in the heavens and on earth: behold, in that are signs indeed for those who reflect. (Qur'an 45:13)*

It is the human family that is addressed in the above and in other verses of the Qur'an. And since that family **includes both genders**, it follows that the basic right to personal possession of property (as Allah's trustees) applies equally to males and females. More specifically:

1. The Shari'ah (Islamic Law) recognizes the full **property rights of women** before and after marriage. They may buy, sell or lease any or all of their properties at will. For this reason, Muslim women may keep (and in fact they have tradition-ally kept) their maiden names after marriage, an indication of their independent property rights as legal entities.[7]

FINANCIAL SECURITY AND INHERITANCE LAWS

2. **Financial security is assured** for women. They are entitled to receive marital gifts without limit and to keep present and future properties and income for their own security, even after marriage. No married woman is required to spend any amount at all from her property and income on the household. In special circumstances, how-ever, such as when her husband is ill, disabled or jobless, she may find it necessary to spend from her earnings or savings to provide the necessities for her family. While this is not a legal obligation, it is consistent with the mutuality of care, love and cooperation among family members. The woman is entitled also to full financial support during mar-riage and during the waiting period (*'iddah*)[8] in case of divorce or widowhood. Some jurists require, in addition, one year's support for divorce and widowhood (or until they remarry, if remar-riage takes place before the year is over).

A woman who bears a child in marriage is entitled to **child support** from the child's father. Generally, a Muslim woman is guaranteed support in all stages of her life, as a daughter, wife, mother or sister. The financial advantages accorded to women, and not to men, in marriage and in family have **a social counterpart** in the provisions that the Qur'an lays down in the laws of **inheritance,** which afford the male, in most cases, twice the inheritance of a female. Males inherit more, but ultimately they are financially responsible for their female relatives: their wives, daughters, mothers and sisters. Females inherit less, but retain their share for investment and financial security, without any legal obligation to spend any part of it, even for their own sustenance (food, clothing, housing, medication, etcetera).

It should be noted that in pre-Islamic society, women themselves were sometimes objects of inheritance (see Qur'an 4:19). In some Western countries, even after the advent of Islam, the whole estate of the deceased was given to his/her eldest son. The Qur'an, however, made it clear that both men and women are entitled to a specified share of the estate of their deceased parents or close relations:

> *From what is left by parents and those*
> *nearest related, there is a share for men and*
> *a share for women, whether the property be*
> *small or large—a determinate share.*
> *(Qur'an 4:7)*

EMPLOYMENT

With regard to the **woman's right to seek employment**, it should be stated first that Islam regards her role in society as a mother and a wife as her most sacred and essential one. Neither maids nor baby-sitters can possibly take the mother's place as the educator of an upright, complex-free, and carefully-reared child. Such a noble and vital role, which largely shapes the future of nations, cannot be regarded as "idleness." This may explain why a married woman must secure her husband's consent if she wishes to work, unless her right to work was mutually agreed to as a condition at the time of marriage.

However, there is no decree in Islam that forbids women from seeking employment whenever there is a necessity for it, especially in positions which fit her nature best and in which society needs her most. Examples of these professions are nursing, teaching (especially children), medicine, and social and charitable work. Moreover, there is no restriction on benefitting from women's talents in any field. Some early jurists, such as Abu-Hanifah and Al-Tabari, uphold that a qualified Muslim woman may be appointed to the position of a judge. Other jurists hold different opinions. Yet, no jurist is able to point to an **explicit text** in the Qur'an or Sunnah that categorically excludes women from any lawful type of employment except for the headship of the state, which is discussed in the following chapter. Omar, the second Caliph after the Prophet (P), appointed a woman

(Um Al-Shifaa' bint Abdullah) as the marketplace supervisor, a position that is equivalent in our world to "director of the consumer protection department."

In countries where Muslims are a numerical minority, some Muslim women, while recognizing the importance of their role as mothers, may be forced to seek employment in order to survive. This is especially true in the case of divorcees and widows, and in the absence of the Islamic financial security measures outlined above.

Chapter Three

THE SOCIAL ASPECT

AS A DAUGHTER

1. The **Qur'an** ended the cruel pre-Islamic practice of **female infanticide,** *wa'd:*

> *When the female (infant) buried alive is*
> *questioned for what crime she was killed. . . .*
> *(Qur'an 81:8-9)*

2. The Qur'an went further to **rebuke the unwelcoming attitude** of some parents upon hearing the news of the birth of a baby girl, instead of a baby boy:

> *When news is brought to one of them of*
> *(the birth of) a female (child), his face dark-*
> *ens and he is filled with inward grief! With*
> *shame he hides himself from his people*
> *because of the bad news he has had! Shall he*
> *retain her on (sufferance and) contempt or*
> *bury her in the dust? Ah! what an evil*
> *(choice) they decide on! (Qur'an 16:58-59)*

3. Parents are duty-bound to **support and show kindness and justice to their daughters**. Prophet Muhammad (P) said,

> *Whosoever has a daughter and does not bury her alive, does not insult her, and does not favor his son over her, Allah will enter him into Paradise. (Ahmad)*

> *Whosoever supports two daughters until they mature, he and I will come on the day of judgment as this (and he pointed with his two fingers held together). (Ahmad)*[9]

4. A crucial aspect in the upbringing of daughters that greatly influences their future is education. **Education is not only a right, but a responsibility,** for all males and females. Prophet Muhammad (P) said, *"Seeking knowledge is mandatory for every Muslim."*[10] The word "Muslim" here is inclusive of both males and females.

AS A WIFE

1. Marriage in Islam is based on **mutual peace, love and compassion**, and not the mere satisfying of human sexual desire.

> *And among His Signs is this, that He created for you mates from among yourselves that you may dwell in tranquillity with them, and He has put love and mercy between your (hearts); verily in that are signs for those who reflect. (Qur'an 30:21)*

> *(He is) the Creator of the heavens and*
> *the earth: He has made for you pairs from*
> *among yourselves and pairs among cattle: by*
> *this means does He multiply you: there is*
> *nothing whatever like unto Him and He is*
> *the One that hears and sees (all things).*
> *(Qur'an 42:11)*

Marriage and Divorce

2. The female has the right to **accept or reject marriage proposals**. Her consent is a prerequisite to the validity of the marital contract, according to the Prophet's teaching. It follows that if an "arranged marriage" means the marrying of a female without her consent, then such a marriage may be annulled if the female so wishes:

> Ibn Abbas reported that a girl came to
> the Messenger of Allah, and she reported
> that her father had forced her to marry with-
> out her consent. The Messenger of God
> gave her the choice ...(between accepting
> the marriage or invalidating it) (Ahmad,
> hadith no. 2469). Another version of the
> report states that "the girl said: 'Actually, I
> accept this marriage, but I wanted to let
> women know that parents have no right to
> force a husband on them.'" (Ibn-Majah)[11]

3. The husband is responsible for the **maintenance, protection, and overall leadership**

(qiwamah) of the family, within the framework of consultation and kindness. The mutuality and complementarity of husband and wife does not mean "subservience" by either party to the other. Prophet Muhammad (P) helped with household chores, although the responsibilities he bore and the issues he faced in his community were immense.

> *The mothers shall give suck to their off-spring for two whole years, if the father desires to complete the term. But he shall bear the cost of their food and clothing on equitable terms. No soul shall have a burden laid on it greater than it can bear. No mother shall be treated unfairly on account of her child, nor father on account of his child. An heir shall be chargeable in the same way. If they both decide on weaning by mutual consent, and after due consultation, there is no blame on them. If you decide on a foster-mother for your offspring, there is no blame on you, provided you pay (the mother) what you offered on equitable terms. But fear Allah and know that Allah sees well what you do. (Qur'an 2:233)*

Prophet Muhammad (P) instructed Muslims regarding women, "I commend you to be kind to women."[12] He said also, "The best of you is the best to his family (wife)."[13] The Qur'an urges husbands to be **kind and considerate to their wives**, even if a wife falls out of favor with her husband or disinclination for her arises within him. It also outlawed the pre-Islamic Arabian practice whereby the stepson of the deceased father was allowed to take possession of his father's widow(s) (inherit them) as if they were part of the estate of the deceased:

> *0 you who believe! You are forbidden to inherit women against their will. Nor should you treat them with harshness, that you may take away part of the marital gift you have given them, except when they have been guilty of open lewdness; on the contrary, live with them on a footing of kindness and equity. If you take a dislike to them, it may be that you dislike a thing through which Allah brings about a great deal of good. (Qur'an 4:19)*

Should **marital disputes** arise, the Qur'an encourages couples to resolve them privately in a spirit of fairness and probity. **Under no circumstances does the Qur'an encourage, allow, or condone family violence or physical abuse.** In extreme cases, and whenever greater harm, such as divorce, is a likely option, it allows for a husband to administer a gentle pat to his wife that causes no physical harm to the body nor leaves any sort of mark. It may serve, in some cases, to bring to the wife's attention the seriousness of her continued unreasonable behavior (refraction), and may be resorted to only after exhausting other steps discussed in endnote 14. If that mild measure is not likely to prevent a marriage from collapsing, as a last measure, it should not be resorted to. Indeed, the Qur'an outlines an enlightened step and a wise approach for the husband and wife to resolve persistent conflict in their marital life: In the event that dispute cannot be resolved equitably between husband and wife, the Qur'an prescribes **mediation** between the parties through family intervention on behalf of both spouses.[14]

5. **Divorce is a last resort,** permissible but not encouraged, for the Qur'an esteems the preservation of faith and the individual's right—male and female alike—to felicity. Forms of marriage dissolution include an enactment based upon mutual agreement, the husband's initiative, the wife's initiative (if part of her marital contract), the court's decision on a wife's initiative (for a legitimate reason), and the wife's initiative without a "cause," provided that she returns her marital gift to her husband (*khul'*, or divestiture).[15]

6. Priority for the **custody** of young children (up to the age of about seven) is given **to the mother**. A child later may choose the mother or father as his or her custodian. Custody questions are to be settled in a manner that balances the interests of both parents and the well-being of the child.[16]

Polygyny

1. **Associating polygyny with Islam,** as if it were introduced by it or is the norm according to its teachings, **is one of the most persistent myths** perpetuated in Western literature and media. No text

in the Qur'an or Sunnah explicitly specifies either monogamy or polygyny as the norm, although demographic data indicates strongly that monogamy is the norm and polygyny the exception.

In almost all countries and on the global level, the numbers of men and women are almost even, with women typically slightly outnumbering men. As such, it is a practical impossibility to regard polygyny as the norm, since it assumes a demographic structure of at least two-thirds females and one third males (or eighty percent females and twenty percent males, if four wives per male is the norm!). No Qur'anic "norm" is based on an impossible assumption.[17] The Qur'an was revealed by Allah, Who is the creator of males and females. Allah created about equal numbers of human males and females. This is His law in the physical world. It follows that His "norms" in the social realm must be consistent with His norms in the physical realm. Only monogamy fits as a universal norm, with polygamy as an exception.

2. Islam did not outlaw polygyny, as did many other peoples and religious communities; rather, it **regulated and restricted** it. It is neither required nor encouraged, but simply permitted and not outlawed. Edward Westermarck gives numerous examples of the sanctioning of polygyny among Jews, Christians and others.[18]

3. The only passage in the Qur'an (4:3) that explicitly addresses polygyny and restricts its practice, in terms of the number of wives permitted and

the requirement of justice between them on the part of the husband, was revealed **after the Battle of Uhud,** in which dozens of Muslims were martyred, leaving behind **widows and orphans**. This seems to indicate that the intent of its continued permissibility, at least in part, is to deal with individual and collective contingencies that may arise from time to time (e. g., imbalances between the number of males and females, created by war). This provides a moral, practical and humane solution to the problems of widows and orphans, who would otherwise surely be more vulnerable in the absence of a husband and father figure in terms of economics, companionship, proper child rearing and other needs.

If you fear that you shall not be able to deal justly with the orphans, marry women of your choice, two or three or four; but if you fear that you shall not be able to deal justly (with them), then only one. . . (Qur'an 4:3)

4. It is critically important to point out with regard to polygyny that **all parties involved have options**. Men may choose to remain monogamous. A proposed second wife may reject the marriage proposal if she does not wish to be party to a polygynous marriage. A prospective first wife may include in her marital contract a condition that her prospective husband shall practice monogamy. If this condition is mutually accepted, it becomes binding on the husband. Should he later violate this condition, his first wife will be entitled to seek divorce with all the financial rights

connected with it. If such a condition was not included in the marital contract, and if the husband marries a second wife, the first wife may seek khul' (divestiture), explained in endnote 15.

While the Qur'an allowed polygyny, it did not allow polyandry (a woman's marriage to multiple husbands). Anthropologically speaking, polyandry is quite rare. Its practice raises thorny problems related to the lineal identity of children and the law of inheritance, both important issues in Islamic law.

In the case of polygyny, the lineal identities of children are not confused. They all have the same father and each of them knows his or her mother. In the case of polyandry, however, only the mother is known for sure. The father could be any of the "husbands" of the same wife. In addition to lineal identity problems, polyandry raises problems relating to inheritance law. For example, which of the children inherits or shares in the estate of a deceased "probable" father?

AS A MOTHER

1. The Qur'an elevates **kindness to parents** (especially mothers) to a status second only to the worship of Allah.

> Your Lord has decreed that you worship none but Him and that you be kind to parents. Whether one or both of them attain old age in your life, say not to them a word of

*contempt nor repel them, but address them
in terms of honor. (Qur' an 17:23)*

*And We have enjoined on every human
being (to be good) to his/her parents: in travail upon travail did his/her mother bear
him/her and in years twain was his/her wean-
ing: (hear the command) "Show gratitude to
Me and to your parents: to Me is (your final)
destiny." (Qur'an 31:14)*

2. Naturally, the Prophet specified this behavior for his followers, rendering to mothers an
unequaled status in human relationships.

A man came to Prophet Muhammad (P)
asking, "0 Messenger of Allah, who among
the people is the most worthy of my good
companionship?" The Prophet (P) said, *"Your
mother"*. The man said, "Then, who is next?"
The Prophet (P) said, *"Your mother."* The
man said, "Then, who is next?" The Prophet
(P) said, *"Your mother."* The man further
asked, "Then who is next?" Only then did the
Prophet (P) say, *"Your father." (Al-Bukhari)* [19].

AS A SISTER IN FAITH (GENERALLY)

1. According to Prophet Muhammad's (P) saying, "Women are but sisters (*shaqa'iq*, or twin
halves) of men." [20] This hadith is a profound statement that directly relates to the issue of human

equality between the genders. If the first meaning of shaqa'iq is adopted, it means that a male is worth one half (of society), with the female worth the other half. Can "one half" be better or bigger than the other half? Is there a more simple but profound physical image of equality? If the second meaning, "sisters," is adopted, it implies the same. The term "sister" is different from "slave" or "master."

2. Prophet Muhammad (P) taught **kindness, care and respect toward women in general** ("I commend you to be kind to women").[21] It is significant that such instruction of the Prophet (P) was among his final instructions and reminders in the "farewell pilgrimage" address given shortly before his passing away.

MODESTY AND SOCIAL INTERACTION

1. There exists a gap between the normative behavior regarding women outlined in the Qur'an and the prevalent reality among Muslims, both as societies in the Muslim world and as communities in the West. Their diverse **cultural practices reflect both ends of the continuum**—the liberal West and the ultra-restrictive regions of the Muslim world. Some Muslims emulate non-Islamic cultures and adopt their modes of dress, unrestricted mixing, and behavior, which influence them and endanger their families' Islamic integrity and strength. On the other hand, in some Muslim cultures undue and excessive

restrictions for women, if not their total seclusion, is believed to be the ideal. Both extremes seem to contradict the normative teachings of Islam and are not consistent with the virtuous, yet participatory, nature of both men and women in society at the time of the Prophet Muhammad (P).

2. The parameters of proper **modesty for males and females** (dress and behavior) are based on revelatory sources (the Qur'an and authentic Sunnah) and, as such, are regarded by believing men and women as divinely-based guidelines with legitimate aims and divine wisdom behind them. They are not male-imposed or socially-imposed restrictions.

3. The near or **total seclusion of women is alien to the prophetic period**. Interpretive problems in justifying seclusion reflect, in part, cultural influences and circumstances in different Muslim countries. There is ample evidence in authentic (sound) hadith supporting this thesis. Women at the Prophet's (P) time and after him participated with men in acts of worship, such as prayers and pilgrimage, in learning and teaching, in the marketplace, in the discussion of public issues (political life), and in the battlefield when necessary.[22]

Chapter Four

THE LEGAL AND POLITICAL ASPECTS

EQUALITY BEFORE THE LAW

1. Both genders are entitled to **equality before the law** and courts of law. Justice is genderless.

According to the Qur'an, men and women receive the same punishment for crimes such as theft (5:38), fornication (24:2),[23] murder and injury (5:45). Women do possess an independent legal entity in financial and other matters. One legal issue is widely misunderstood: testimony. A common but erroneous belief is that as a "rule," the **worth of women's testimony** is one half of men's testimony. A survey of all passages in the Qur'an relating to testimony does not substantiate this claimed "rule."

Testimony

Most Qur'anic references to testimony (witness) do not make any reference to gender. Some references fully equate the testimony of males and females.

> *And for those who launch a charge*
> *against their spouses and have (in support) no*
> *evidence but their own, their solitary evidence*

*(can be received) if they bear witness four
times (with an oath) by Allah that they are
solemnly telling the truth; And the fifth (oath)
(should be) that they solemnly invoke the curse
of Allah on themselves if they tell a lie. But it
would avert the punishment from the wife if
she bears witness four times (with an oath) by
Allah that (her husband) is telling a lie; And
the fifth (oath) should be that she solemnly
invokes the wrath of Allah on herself if (her
accuser) is telling the truth. (Qur'an 24:6-9)*

One reference in the Qur'an distinguishes
between the witness of a male and a female. It is
useful to quote this reference and explain it in its
own context, and in the context of other Qur'anic
references to testimony:

*0 you who believe! When you deal with
each other in transactions involving future
obligations in a fixed period of time, reduce
them to writing. Let a scribe write down faithfully as between the parties: let not the scribe
refuse to write: as Allah has taught him, so let
him write. Let him who incurs the liability
dictate, but let him fear his Lord, Allah, and
not diminish aught of what he owes. If the
party liable is mentally deficient, or weak, or
unable himself to dictate, let his guardian
dictate faithfully. And get two witnesses out
of your own men, and if there are not two
men, then a man and two women, such as
you choose for witnesses so that if one of*

them errs, the other can remind her. The wit-
nesses should not refuse when they are
called on (for evidence). Disdain not to
reduce to writing (your contract) for a future
period, whether it be small or big: it is more
just in the sight of Allah, more suitable as
evidence, and more convenient to prevent
doubts among yourselves, but if it be a trans-
action which you carry out on the spot among
yourselves, there is no blame on you if you
reduce it not to writing. But take witnesses
whenever you make a commercial contract;
and let neither scribe nor witness suffer
harm. If you do (such harm), it would be
wickedness in you. So fear Allah; for it is
Allah that teaches you. And Allah is well
acquainted with all things. (Qur'an 2:282)

A few comments on this text are essential in order to prevent common misinterpretations:

a. It cannot be used as an argument that there is a general rule in the Qur'an that the worth of a female's witness is only half the male's. This presumed "rule" is voided by the above reference (24:6-9), which **explicitly equates the testimony of both genders** on the issue at hand.

b. The context of this passage (verse, or *ayah*) relates to testimony on financial transactions, which are often complex and laden with business jargon. **The passage does not a make blanket generalization** that would otherwise contradict 24:6-9, cited above.

c. The reason for **variations in the number of male and female witnesses** required is given in the same passage. **No reference is made to the inferiority or superiority of one gender's witness or the other's**. The only reason given is to corroborate the female's witness and prevent unintended errors in the perception of the business deal. The Arabic term used in this passage, *tadhilla*, literally means "loses the way," "gets confused," or "errs." But are females the only gender that may err and need corroboration of their testimony? Definitely not, and that is why the general rule of testimony in Islamic law is to have two witnesses, even when they are both male.

One **possible interpretation** of the requirements related to this particular type of testimony is that in numerous societies, past and present, women generally may not be heavily involved with and experienced in business transactions. As such, they may not be completely cognizant of what is involved. Therefore, corroboration of a woman's testimony by another woman who may be present **ascertains accuracy and, hence, justice**. It would be unreasonable to interpret this requirement as a reflection on the worth of women's testimony, as it is the **only** exception discerned from the text of the Qur'an. This may be one reason why a great scholar like Al-Tabari could not find any evidence from any primary text (Qur'an or hadith) to exclude women from something **more important than testimony: being herself a judge who hears and evaluates the testimony of others.**

d. It must be added that unlike pure acts of worship, which must be observed exactly as taught by the Prophet (P), testimony is a **means to an end, ascertaining justice** as a major objective of Islamic law. Therefore, it is the duty of a fair judge to be guided by this objective when assessing the worth and credibility of a given testimony, regardless of the gender of the witness. A witness of a female graduate of a business school is certainly far more worthy than the witness of an illiterate person with no business education or experience.

PARTICIPATION IN SOCIAL AND POLITICAL LIFE

2. The **general rule in social and political life is participation and collaboration** of males and females in public affairs.

> The believers, men and women, are pro-
> tectors, one of another: they enjoin what is
> just and forbid what is evil: they observe reg-
> ular prayers, practice regular charity, and
> obey Allah and His apostle. On them will
> Allah pour His mercy: for Allah is Exalted in
> power, Wise. (Qur'an 9:7)

3. There is sufficient **historical evidence of participation** by Muslim women in the choice of rulers, in public issues, in lawmaking, in administrative positions, in scholarship and teaching, and even in the battlefield. Such involvement in social

and political affairs was conducted without the participants losing sight of the complementary priorities of both genders, and without violating Islamic guidelines of modesty and virtue.

WOMEN IN LEADERSHIP POSITIONS

There is no text in the Qur'an or Sunnah that precludes women from any position of **leadership**, except in leading prayer (however, women may lead other women in prayer), due to the format of prayer, as explained earlier. There are exceptions even to this general rule, as explained later in this chapter. Another common question relates to the eligibility of Muslim women to be heads of state.

There is no evidence from the Qur'an to preclude women from headship of state. Some may argue that according to the Qur'an (4:34), men are the protectors and maintainers of women. Such a leadership position (responsibility, or *qiwamah*) for men in the family unit implies their exclusive leadership in political life as well. This analogy, however, is far from conclusive. Qiwamah deals with the particularity of family life and the need for financial arrangements, role differentiation, and complementarity of the roles of husband and wife. These particularities are not necessarily the same as the headship of state, even if some elements may be similar. Therefore, a Qur'anically-based argument to exclude women from the headship of state is neither sound nor convincing. Most arguments for exclusion, however, are based on the following hadith, narrated by Abu Bakrah:

During the battle of Al-Jamal (in which A'isha, the Prophet's widow, led an army in opposition to Ali, the fourth Caliph), Allah benefitted me with a word. When the Prophet heard the news that the people of Persia had made the daughter of Khosrau their queen (ruler), he said, *"Never will such a nation succeed as makes a woman their ruler."*[24]

While this hadith has been commonly interpreted to exclude women from the headship of state, other scholars **do not agree with that interpretation**. The Persian rulers at the time of the Prophet (P) showed enmity toward the Prophet (P) and toward his messenger to them. The Prophet's response to this news may have been a statement about the impending doom of that unjust empire, which did take place later, and not about the issue of gender as it relates to headship of the state in itself. Z. Al-Qasimi argues that one of the rules of interpretation known to Muslim scholars is that there are cases in which the determining factor in interpretation is the **specificity of the occasion** (of the hadith), and **not the generality of its wording**. Even if the generality of its wording is to be accepted, that does not necessarily mean that a general rule is applicable, **categorically**, to any situation. As such, the hadith is not conclusive evidence of categorical exclusion.[25]

Some argue that since women are excluded from leading the prayer for a mixed gathering of men and women, they should be excluded from leading the state as well. This argument, however, overlooks two issues: (1) Leading the prayer is a purely religious act, and given the format of Muslim prayer and its nature, it is not suitable for women to lead a mixed congregation. This point was discussed earlier. Leading the state, however, is not a "purely" religious act, but a religiously-based **political** act. Exclusion of women in one instance does not necessarily imply their exclusion in another.[26] (2) Even the matter of whether women may lead prayer is not without exception. Prophet Muhammad (P) asked a woman by the name of Umm Waraqah to lead her household in prayer, which included a young girl, a young boy, and a mu'azzin (caller to prayer—who is always a male).[27]

Al-Qasimi notes that the famous jurist, Abu-Ya'la Al-Farra' (known for his writings on the political system of Islam), did not include among the qualifications of the imam (head of state) being a male.[28] It should be noted, however, that the head of state in Islam is **not a ceremonial head.** He leads public prayers on some occasions, and constantly travels and negotiates with officials of other states (who generally are men). He may be involved in confidential meetings with them. Such heavy and secluded involvement of women with men and its necessary format may not be consistent with Islamic guidelines related to the proper interaction between the genders, and to the priority of feminine functions at home and their value to society.

Furthermore, the **conceptual and philosophical background** of the critics of this limited exclusion is that of individualism, ego satisfaction, and the rejection of the validity of divine guidance in favor of other man-made philosophies, values or "isms." The ultimate objective of a Muslim man or woman, however, is to selflessly serve Allah and the Ummah in whatever appropriate capacity. In the incident of Al-Hudaybiyah, Umm Salamah, a wife of the Prophet (P), played a role equal to what we would refer to today as "chief advisor of the head of state."

Conclusion

THE IDEAL AND THE REALITY

ISLAMIC REFORMATION AND RENEWAL

This work focuses on the **normative,** or ideal, relating to gender equity in Islam. This ideal may serve as a yardstick against which the **reality** of present-day Muslims should be evaluated. It serves also as the objective toward which any **Islamic reformation and renewal** should be directed, reformation of wrong practices and renewal of adherence to the Islamic ideal.

When assessing the realities of Muslims, two extremes should be avoided:

1. Justifying injustices done to most Muslim women by **religiously-flavored cultural arguments**

Most problematic in that extreme is the subtle **assumption** of the "correctness" of traditional cultural practices and attitudes, followed by a **selective** search for endorsement in the primary sources of Islam.

2. Failing to see numerous **positive aspects** in Muslim societies, such as family stability and cohesiveness, the respect and adoration of mothers, and the sense of self-fulfillment of women who are not frequently seen in public; in the meantime, painting a **stereotypical picture of Muslim women** as ignorant, submissive, oppressed and almost totally enslaved by women-hating chauvinist men

The focus on injustices and on magnifying them is sometimes partly based on questionable interpretations of outsiders' observations. For example, the smaller percentage of career women in many Muslim societies is interpreted in a **Western framework**, and is seen as an indication of Muslims' oppressing women and depriving them of job opportunities. Little attention, if any, is given to the **personal choices of Muslim women and their concepts of family happiness**, which may or may not be the same choices or concepts of their non-Muslim sisters.

RELATING TO INTERNATIONAL BODIES AND MOVEMENTS

Once an objective and fair assessment of Muslim practices is made, it should be compared with the normative teachings of Islam. There are enough indications to show that a gap **does** exist between the ideal and the real. Given the existence of such a gap, a wide gap at times, it follows that Muslim reformers and other international bodies and movements **share at least one thing in common**: an awareness of the need to close, or at least narrow, that gap. The problem arises, however, as to the most effective frame of reference and to the particulars of implementation.

International bodies and women's rights organizations tend to consider **documents and resolutions passed in conferences** as the ultimate basis and standard expected of all diverse peoples, cultures and religions. Committed Muslims, however, both men and women, believe in the ultimate supremacy of what they accept as **God's divine revelation** (the Qur'an and authentic hadith). To tell Muslims that one's religious convictions should be subservient to "superior" man-made (or woman-made) standards or to secular humanism, is neither acceptable nor practical. Even if pressures, **economic and otherwise,** are used to bring about compliance with such resolutions or documents, the resulting changes are not likely to be **deep-rooted and lasting**. For Muslims, divine injunctions and guidance are not subject to a "voting" procedure or to human election, editing, or whimsical modifications. They constitute, rather, a complete way of living within Islam's spiritual, moral, social, political and legal parameters. Imposed cultural imperialism is not the solution.

IMPOSITION OR REFORM FROM WITHIN

On the other hand, reformation from within requires the following:

1. Social scientists, legislators and rulers should avoid using the argument of **cultural particularity** to justify anti-Islamic and non-Islamic practices and to **continue oppressing men and women alike.**

2. Scholars should not continue to quote and repeat some of the long-standing **juristic interpretations** as if they were equal in authority and finality to the two primary sources of Islam. Nor

should they engage in a **fragmentary and selective approach in seeking justification** of the erroneous status quo. They should realize that even the greatest of jurists are fallible humans, whose interpretations have been affected by the culture and circumstances under which they have lived. With the host of pressing and significant contemporary issues, a fresh *ijtihad* (interpretation) is needed.

One of the main obstacles in the way of such a reexamination of some of the traditional views is worry on the part of some scholars about the reaction of other scholars or of the public to their conclusions. Yet, it is not the duty of the scholar to speak for what others want or expect. A qualified scholar is duty-bound to give **practical answers to contemporary issues and problems**, without losing sight of the boundaries of proper interpretation. In the final analysis, it is Muslims' **practices and understanding that need revision, not the revelatory sources, if properly understood, and more important, implemented.**

Appendix

IS FEMALE CIRCUMCISION REQUIRED?

A common **misconception** is to connect female circumcision with the teachings of Islam. This appendix addresses the following three questions:

1. WAS FEMALE CIRCUMCISION INTRODUCED BY ISLAM?

While the exact origin of female circumcision is not known, **"it preceded Christianity and Islam."**[1] The most radical form of female circumcision (infibulation) is known as the **Pharaonic** Procedure. This may signify that it may have been practiced long before the rise of Islam, Christianity and possibly Judaism. It is not clear, however, whether this practice originated in Egypt, or in some other African countries, and then spread to Egypt.[2]

---

[1] Stewart, Rosemary, "Female Circumcision: Implications for North American Nurses," in *Journal of Psychosocial Nursing*, vol. 35, no. 4, 1997, p. 35.

[2] *Haqa'iq Ilmiyya Hawla Khitan Al-Inaath* (in Arabic), Jam'iyyat Tanzeem Al-Usrah, Cairo, 1983, p. 7.

It is common knowledge that in some countries like Egypt, female circumcision has been **practiced by both Muslims** and Christians.[3] In the meantime, this practice is not known in most Muslim countries, including Iraq, Iran, and Saudi Arabia.[4] This leads to the conclusion that **female circumcision is connected** with **cultural practices, rather than with Islam itself** as a world religion. It was made clear in the introduction of this book that some cultural practices, whether by Muslims alone, or Muslims and others (such as the case with female circumcision), are not part of Islam, and in some instances, may violate its teachings as embodied in its **primary sources,** Qur'an and hadith. These sources are examined next.

2. Is There Any Authentic Text in the Primary Sources of Islam Which Requires Female Circumcision for Religious Reasons?

No **mention** of female circumcision is to be found **in the Qur'an**, either directly or indirectly. There is **no known hadith which requires female circumcision.** Some argued, however, that one hadith, while not requiring female circumcision, appears to accept it: "Circumcision is a commendable act for men (Sunnah) and an honorable thing for women (Makromah)."[5]

---

[3] *Ibid*, p. 8.

[4] *Ibid*, p. 8.

[5] Al-Shawkani, *Nayl Al-Awtar*, Dar Al-Jeel, Beirut, 1973, vol. 1, p. 139.

There are two observations on this hadith:

a) A distinction is made between male circumcision, which is described in a stronger religious term (Sunnah),[6] or commendable, while another **weaker description is given** to female circumcision (Makromah), which implies **no religious obligation.**

b) This hadith is of **weak authenticity** (dha'eef), according to hadith scholars.[7]

There is, however, a more authentic hadith, in which Prophet Muhammad (P) is reported to have passed by a woman performing circumcision on a young girl. He instructed the woman by saying:

> "Cut off only the foreskin (outer fold of skin over the clitoris; the prepuce) but do not cut off deeply (i.e. the clitoris itself), for this is brighter for the face (of the girl) and more favorable with the husband."[8]

---

[6] A broader definition of Sunnah is "the words, actions and approval (or consent) of Prophet Muhammad (P)." In the context of religious obligations, however, Sunnah refers to acts that are commendable, but not obligatory. It is in that context that the Prophet Muhammad (P) used the term Sunnah to refer to male circumcision, but not female circumcision.

[7] Al-Shawkani, op. cit, p. 139.

[8] Al-Tabarani, quoted in Al-Albani, Muhammad N., *Silsilat Al-Ahadeeth Al-Sahihah*, Al-Maktab Al-Islami, Beirut, Lebanon, 1983, vol. 2, Hadith no. 722, pp. 353-358 especially pp. 356-357. See also N. Keller (translator/editor), *The Reliance of the Traveller* by Ahmad Al-Masri, Modern Printing Press, Dubai, 1991, e 4.3, p. 59.

While the Prophet (P) did not explicitly ban this practice, his words project a great deal of **sensitivity to the instinctive needs of females and their matrimonial happiness** and legitimate enjoyment. Reference to the brightness of the face and to a better relationship with the husband are clear indications of the Prophet (P)'s sensitivity and compassion. His teaching also stands in contrast to the arguments that female circumcision "controls" the woman's sexual appetite and hence contributes to sexual morality and virtue in society. It is true that **Islam requires adherents of both genders to be chaste**. Yet, there is no text in the Qur'an or Sunnah which requires **selective curtailment** or control of the sexual desire of one specific gender. Furthermore, chastity and virtue are not contingent on "cutting off" part of any sensitive and crucial human organ. Rather, they are contingent on spiritual and **moral values** of the person and the supporting virtuous environments.

3. SHOULD FEMALE CIRCUMCISION BE BANNED OR RESTRICTED?

Shari'ah (Islamic law) divides actions into five categories; mandatory, commendable, permissible, detestable, and strictly forbidden. Female circumcision falls within the **category of the permissible**. It was probably on this basis that some scholars opposed **a sweeping ban** of this practice. Before discussing this view, it is important to distinguish between different types of procedures that were, and still are, called circumcision.

TYPES OF CIRCUMCISION

a) Removal of the hood (or prepuce) of the clitoris. This procedure is, to some degree, **analogous to male circumcision** since in both cases, no part of the sexual organ is cut off. In both cases also, it is only the foreskin, or outer fold of the skin, which is cut off. Properly done, it is not likely to cause any "matrimonial" problem. While some may call it "sunnah circumcision," this is their own appellation and not that of the Prophet (P), who used the term Sunnah only in the context of male circumcision.

b) Removal of the entire clitoris (clitorectomy), along with part of the labia minora, which is sutured together, leaving an opening. This is a form of **mutilation.**

c) Removal of the entire clitoris, labia minora and medial part of the labia majora, with both sides of the female organ stitched together, leaving a small opening. This procedure requires tying together the child's legs for nearly three weeks.[9] It is called the Pharaonic procedure, but **may as well be called "mutilation."**

It is obvious that the **second and third procedures were never mandated, encouraged or even consented to by the Prophet (P).** They even violate a known rule in Shari'ah prohibiting the cutting off

---

[9] Stewart, *op. cit*, p. 35.

of any part of the human body except for unavoidable reasons (e.g. medical treatment, trimming nails or hair, or for an explicitly specified reason such as male circumcision). Such necessity or need does not exist in female circumcision. **Nothing justifies genital mutilation. In fact, no mutilation is allowed by Islam, even in the battlefield.** Not only are these two procedures unjustifiable, they are brutal, inhumane and in violation of Islam.

The remaining question then relates to the first procedure. Some (e.g. the late Rector of Al-Azhar University, Sheikh Gad Al-Haque) argued that since the Prophet (P) did not ban female circumcision, it falls within the category of the permissible. As such, there is no ground for a total ban on it. However, it is within the spirit of Shari'ah to **restrict something that is permissible if discovered to be harmful.** For example, all fish are permissible to be eaten. Should a particular type of fish be proven to be poisonous or harmful, it could be banned based on a known Shari'ah rule (Al-dharar Yozaal), or the harm must be removed. The real issue then boils down to **whether the first procedure is harmful or not.** Granted that such a procedure may not be seriously damaging like the other two, it may be argued that it is **painful, traumatic and often performed in an unhygienic setting,** leading to infection and other problems.[10]

---

[10] Including bleeding, scars, painful intercourse, difficulty to achieve sexual fulfillment which may lead to pain, reducing chances of pregnancy, causing infertility in some instances, chronic pelvic infection, urinary tract infection, psychological problems, and unhappy husbands. See Stewart, *op. cit*, pp. 36-37.

Even if the procedure is performed by a physician, it is so delicate that not all physicians master it.[11]

It should be noted that some people oppose female circumcision as part of their opposition to any "tradition" as old and invalid. This is as inappropriate as practicing female circumcision because it is a "tradition," regardless of its consistency with Islam or not. The practice should be **evaluated objectively**, on the basis of

a) whether it is **required** religiously or not

b) whether there are **medical and other** relevant issues to be considered in evaluating this practice.

While any form of female circumcision is already legally banned in some countries[12] and may be banned in others in the future, it is not suggested here that this is the **only option**. In societies and cultures where the practice is well-entrenched, and sociocultural pressures for it are great[13],

---

[11] The author was informed by some physicians that since the clitoris itself is quite tiny, even tinier in younger girls, it is very difficult to do the first procedure properly, even by a non-specialist physician. The much easier procedure of male circumcision is usually referred to a physician with experience in that particular procedure.

[12] Presently female circumcision is illegal in Britain and other European countries through the passage of the Prohibition of Female Circumcision Act of 1985. Due to the publicity given to this topic recently, other countries are expected to follow suit, especially those with a large number of immigrants from countries which practice this procedure. Stewart, *op. cit*, p. 36.

[13] Some of such pressure is based on the *non-Islamically-based* cultural norms that only a circumcised woman is fit for marriage, and on other superstitious ideas, including that a child born to an uncircumcised woman is likely to die. See for example Stewart, *op. cit*, p. 36.

abrupt legal banning may not end the practice. It may cause it to be practiced "underground," and under more problematic circumstances. However, the **problem is serious enough** that some action is needed. A starting point, perhaps, is to begin by **educating the masses** in countries where female circumcision is commonly practiced. All possible media should be used in the process. The contents of this appendix may serve as an outline of such an educational program, or it is so hoped. In any case, the conclusion which appears to be certain is that **there is no single text of the Qur'an** and **hadith which requires**[14] **female circumcision**.

---

[14] Reference is sometimes made to a saying of the Prophet Muhammad (P) narrated in Ahmad, also in Malik with similar wordings, to the effect that if the two areas of circumcision (for a male and female) touch one another, then Ghusl (bathing) is required. This expression simply signifies that after the intimate matrimonial relationship, both husband and wife must take a complete bath before they perform their daily prayers. The relevant part of this hadith, however, is its reference to the *two* circumcised parts. Imam Ahmad uses this hadith as an evidence that women (in Madinah) used to be circumcised. This is no evidence, however, that it was religiously required. It could have been a cultural practice which was not prohibited.

Even the few ahadith which Al-Albani considered to be authentic do not require female circumcision, as discussed earlier. In fact, some of them speak against radical forms of circumcision.

See Sabiq, Al-Sayyid, *Fiqh Al-Sunnah,* Dar Al-Kitab Al-Arabi, Beirut, 1969, vol. 1, pp. 37 and 66. Also Al-Albani, Muhammad N., *Tamam Al-Minnah Fi Al-Ta'leeq Ala Fiqh Al-Sunnah,* Al-Maktabah Al-Islamiyyah, Amman, 3rd printing, 1409 A.H., p. 67, and *Muwatta'Al-Imam Malik* , Dar Al-Qalam, Beirut, n.d., pp. 50-51.

Notes

ix   ¹ The term "equity" is used instead of the more common expression "equality," which is sometimes misunderstood to mean absolute equality in each and every detailed item of comparison, rather than overall equality. *Equity* is used here to mean justice and overall equality in the totality of rights and responsibilities of both genders and allows for the possibility of variations in specific items within the **overall balance and equality**. It is analogous to two persons possessing diverse currencies amounting, for each person, to the equivalent of US $1000. While each of the two persons may possess more of one currency than the other, the total value still comes to US $1000 in each case. It should be added that from an Islamic perspective, the roles of men and women are **complementary and cooperative**, rather than competitive.

1   ² The **Qur'an** is universally accepted by Muslims as the word of Allah, or "God," dictated verbatim to Prophet Muhammad (P) through Angel Gabriel. It is divided into 114 units, each called a *surah*. The Qur'an is the **highest authority** for information on Islam. **Sunnah** refers to the words, actions and confirmations (consent) of Prophet Muhammad (P) in matters pertaining to the meaning and practice of Islam. Another common term that some authorities consider to be equivalent to *Sunnah* is **hadith** (plural *ahadith*), which literally means "sayings."

The letter (P) is an abbreviation of "peace be upon him," a form of respect used by Muslims whenever the name of any prophet is mentioned.

6   3 In both Qur'anic references, 15:28 and 32:7, the Arabic terms used are *basharan* and *al-insaan*. Both mean a **human being or a person**. English translations do not usually convey this meaning and commonly use the terms "man" or the pronoun "him" to refer to "person," which is actually without a particular gender identification. Equally erroneous is the common translation of "*bani-Adam*" as "sons of Adam" or "men" instead of the more accurate translation, "children of Adam."

8   4 The explanatory "**both**" was added whenever the Qur'anic Arabic text addresses Adam and Eve, as in "*lahoma, akala, akhrajahoma*." This was done in order to avoid misinterpreting the English term "you" to mean an address to a singular person. For the Biblical version of the story and its implications, see The Bible, RSV, American Bible Society, N.Y.,1952, Genesis, chs. 2-3, especially 3:6, 12, 16-17; Leviticus 12:1-7 and 15:19-30, and Timothy 2:11-14. It may be added here that in one surah in the Qur'an it is Adam, not Eve, who is especially chastised for eating from the "forbidden tree," even through Eve is not regarded as totally blameless:

> *We (Allah) had already, beforehand*
> *taken the covenant of Adam, but he forgot:*
> *and We found no firm resolve on his part.*
> *(Qur'an 20:115)*

After relating the story of temptation and the partaking of the "forbidden tree," the Qur'an states,

> . . . *Thus did Adam disobey His Lord,*
> *and allow himself to be seduced (by Satan).*
> *(Qur'an 20:121)*

9   5   Pregnancy and childbirth are not the only feminine functions that are treated with respect and compassion. The same applies to menstruation. In consideration of the health of husband and wife and to prevent discomfort to the wife, sexual intercourse is prohibited during menstruation. This is what is meant by the Qur'anic directive,

> *They ask you [O Muhammad] concern-*
> *ing menstruation. Say: It is a hurt and a*
> *pollution. So keep away from women (i.e.*
> *do not engage in intercourse with them)*
> *until they are clean. . . (Qur'an 2:222)*

Two common misunderstandings of this passage need to be cleared:

a. The description of "pollution" does **not apply to women** but to menstrual blood. Not only is it unhealthy to engage in intercourse during this period, but it may also hurt the woman due to the irritation that may be caused by such an activity.

b. The restriction here is limited to intercourse, not to any other forms of permissible sexual intimacy, as is clearly explained in hadith. Keeping away from

women **does not mean "do not touch them**, sit or eat
with them," or even "do not be intimate with them."
Prophet Muhammad (P) used to rest his head on
A'isha's lap during her menses and recite the Qur'an,
perform his prayers very close to her, let her comb
his hair, drink from the same cup she drank from,
and allow her to bring things he needed from the
mosque. Numerous ahadith to this effect are narrated by Bukhari and Muslim. See Abu-Shuqqah,
Tahrir Al-Mar'ah Al-Muslimah Fi 'Asr Al-Risalah (in
Arabic), Dar Al-Qalam, Kuwait, vol 6, pp. 107-109.

13   6 A common question raised in the West is whether a
Muslim woman can be ordained as a minister, as
more liberal churches allow. It should be remem-
bered that there is no "church" or **"priesthood"** in
Islam. The question of "ordination" therefore
does not arise. However, most of the common
"priestly" functions, such as religious education
and spiritual and social counseling, are not forbidden to Muslim women in a proper Islamic context.
Woman, however, may not lead prayers (except
for other women), as Muslim prayers involve pros-
trations and body contact. Since the prayer leader
is supposed to stand in front of the congregation
and may move forward in the middle of crowded
rows, it would be both inappropriate Islamically
and uncomfortable for a female to be in such a
position and prostrate, hands, knees and forehead
on the ground, with rows of men behind her. A
Muslim **female** may be an Islamic **scholar**. In the
history of Islam, there were many examples of
female scholars who taught both genders.

16 [7] This contrasts with the legal provisions in Europe, which did not recognize that right until nearly **thirteen centuries after Islam**. In Britain, "by a series of acts starting with the Married Women's Property Act in 1870, amended in 1882 and 1887, married women achieved the right to own property and to enter into contracts on a par with spinsters, widows and divorcees." See *Encyclopedia Britannica*, 1968, vol. 23, p. 624.

16 [8] This period is usually three months. If the wife is pregnant, it extends until childbirth. In the case of widows, the waiting period is 130 days. In case of divorce before a marriage is consummated, there is no required waiting period, and the woman may remarry immediately after divorce (Qur'an 33:49).

22 [9] Ahmad Ibn-Hanbal (compiler), *Musnad Ibn Hanbal*, Dar Al- Ma'arif, Cairo, Egypt, 1950 and 1955, vol. 3 and 4, ahadith 1957 and 2104.

22 [10] Narrated in Al-Bayhaqi and Ibn-Majah, quoted in M.S. Afifi, *Al-Mar'ah Wa Huququha Fil-Islam* (in Arabic), Maktabat Al-Nahdhah, Cairo, Egypt, 1988, p. 71.

23 [11] Ibn Majah (compiler), *Sunan Ibn Majah*, Dar Ihya' Al Kutub Al-Arabiyyah, Cairo, Egypt, 1952, vol.1, hadith 1873.

24 [12] *Matn Al-Bukhari*, Dar Ihya' Al-Kutub Al-Arabiyyah, Cairo, Egypt, n.d., vol.3, p. 257.

24   [13] *Riyadh Al-Saliheen*, (Al-Nawawi, Compiler), Nizamuddin, New Delhi, India, n.d., p. 140.

26   [14] In the event of a family dispute, the Qur'an exhorts the husband to treat his wife kindly and not overlook her **positive aspects** (see Qur'an 4:19). If the problem relates to the wife's behavior, her husband may exhort her and appeal for reason. In most cases, this measure is likely to be sufficient. In cases where the problem continues, the husband may express his displeasure in another peaceful manner, by sleeping in a separate bed from hers. There are cases, however, in which a wife persists in deliberate mistreatment and expresses contempt of her husband and disregard for her marital obligations. Instead of divorce, the husband may resort to another measure that may save the marriage, at least in some cases. Such a measure is more accurately described as a gentle tap on the body, but **never on the face**, making it more of a symbolic measure than a punitive one. Following is the related Qur'anic text:

> *Men are the protectors and maintainers of women, because Allah has given the one more (strength) than the other, and because they support them from their means. Therefore the righteous women are devoutly obedient, and guard in (the husband's) absence what Allah would have them guard. As to those women on whose part you fear disloyalty and ill-conduct, admonish them (first), (next) do not share their*

beds, (and last) beat (tap) them (lightly); but
if they return to obedience, seek not against
them means (of annoyance): for Allah is
Most High, Great (above you all). (4:34)

Even here, that maximum measure is limited
by the following:

a. It must be seen as **a rare exception to the
repeated exhortation of mutual respect, kindness
and good treatment**, discussed earlier. Based on
the Qur'an and hadith, this measure may be used
in the cases of lewdness on the part of the wife, or
extreme refraction and rejection of the husband's
reasonable requests on a consistent basis
(*nushuz*). Even then, other measures, such as
exhortation, should be tried first.

b. As defined by hadith, it is **not permissible
to strike anyone's face, cause any bodily harm or
even be harsh**. What the hadith qualified as
dharban ghayra mubarrih, or light striking, was
interpreted by early jurists as a (symbolic) use of
the miswak (a small natural toothbrush)! They
further qualified permissible "striking" as that
which leaves no mark on the body. It is interesting that this latter fourteen-centuries-old qualifier
is the criterion used in contemporary American
law to separate a light and harmless tap or strike
from "abuse" in the legal sense. This makes it
clear that even this extreme, last resort, and "less-
er of the two evils" measure that may save a marriage does not meet the definitions of "physical
abuse," "family violence," or "wife battering" in the

20th-century law in liberal democracies, where such extremes are so commonplace that they are seen as national concerns.

    c.   The permissibility of such symbolic expression of the seriousness of continued refraction **does not imply its desirability**. In several ahadith, Prophet Muhammad (P) discouraged this measure. Among his sayings are the following: *"Do not beat the female servants of Allah;" "Some (women) visited my family complaining about their husbands (beating them). These (husbands) are not the best of you;"* and *"[Is it not a shame that] one of you beats his wife like [an unscrupulous person] beats a slave and maybe he sleeps with her at the end of the day."* (See *Riyadh Al-Saliheen,*op.cit, p.p. 137-140). In another hadith, the Prophet (P) said,

    . . . How does anyone of you beat his wife as he beats the stallion camel and then he may embrace (sleep with) her? . . . (Sahih Al-Bukhari, op. cit., vol. 8, hadith 68, pp. 42-43).

    d.   True following of the Sunnah is to follow the example of Prophet Muhammad (P), who **never resorted to that measure,** regardless of the circumstances.

    e.   Islamic teachings are universal in nature. They respond to the needs and circumstances of **diverse times, cultures and circumstances**. Some measures may work in some cases and cultures or with certain persons, but may not be effective in others. By definition, a "permissible" act is neither required, encouraged or forbidden. In fact, it may be **better to spell out the extent** of permissibility, such as in the issue at hand, rather than leaving it unrestricted and unqualified, or ignoring it all together. In the absence of strict qualifiers, persons may interpret the matter in their own way, which can lead to excesses and real abuse.

f. Any excess, cruelty, family violence, or abuse committed by any "Muslim" can never be traced, honestly, to any revelatory text (Qur'an or hadith). Such **excesses and violations are to be blamed on the person(s) himself**, as it shows that they are paying lip service to Islamic teachings and injunctions and failing to follow the true Sunnah of the Prophet (P).

26   [15] Khul', or divestiture, is an arrangement whereby the wife may offer some financial compensation to her husband (usually by returning his marital gift to him), in return for terminating the marital relationship. It is provided for in cases in which there is **"no fault"** on the part of the husband (e.g. failure to support his wife, impotence or abuse) and **the wife is the one who initiates** marriage dissolution. In such cases, it is only fair that she should return to her husband whatever he gave or paid her with the view of permanent and lasting marital commitment. In case of dispute over the amount of compensation, a judge may examine the case and

determine the fair amount, which is normally the marital gift (mahr) previously paid by the husband. See Sayyid Sabiq's *Fiqh-us-Sunnah*, Dar Al-Kitab Al-Arabi, Beirut, Lebanon, 1969, pp. 294-308.

26   [16] For more details on marriage dissolution and custody of children, see H. Abd al-Ati, *Family Structure in Islam*, American Trust Publications, Indianapolis, In, 1977, pp. 217-249; Sayyid Sabiq, *Fiqh-us-Sunnah*, ibid., vol. 2, p. 349.

27   [17] For more details on the issue of polygyny, see Badawi, Jamal.A, *Polygyny In Islamic Law*, American Trust Publications, Indianapolis, IN; also *Islamic Teachings* (audio series), Islamic Information Foundation, Halifax, Canada, 1982, album 4. The term *polygyny*, rather than *polygamy*, is used since *polygamy* means either polygyny (more than one wife of the same husband), or polyandry (more than one husband of the same wife). Only polygyny is permissible in Islam.

27   [18] See, for example, Westermarck, Edward A., *The History of Human Marriage*, (5th Edition Rewritten), Macmillan and Co., London, 1925, vol. 3, pp. 42-43; also *Encyclopedia Biblica* (Rev. T.K. Cheney and S. Black, Editiors), Macmillan, London, 1925, vol 3, p. 2946.

30   [19] *Matn Al-Bukhari,* op. cit., vol. 4, kitab Al-Adab, p. 47. Translated by the author. For a similar English translation of this hadith, see *Sahih Al-Bukhari*, translated by M.M. Khan, Maktabat Al-Riyadh Al-

Hadeethah, Riyadh, Saudi Arabia, 1982, vol. 8, "The Book of Al-Adab," hadith 2, p. 2.

30 [20] Narrated by A'isha (R.A.), collected by Ibn 'Asakir in *Silsilat Kunuz Al Sunnah I, Al-Jami' Al-Sagheer*, 1st ed., 1410 A.H. (after Hijrah). Computer software.

31 [21] *Riyadh Al-Saliheen*, op.cit., p.139.

32 [22] For a comprehensive and detailed documentation from the most authentic sources of hadith, see Abdul Haleem Abu-Shuqqah, *Tahrir Al-Mar'ah* op. cit., 1990, 91, 94, vols. 1-6.

33 [23] An earlier passage in the Qur'an (4:15-16) appears to prescribe a different punishment for lewdness in the cases of females and males (confinement at the home for the guilty female and unspecified punishment for the guilty male, without requiring his confinement at home). Al-Razi suggests that since the male was the breadwinner of the family, confining him at home would thus punish his innocent dependents. A female, on the other hand, is always guaranteed support, making her confinement a personal punishment only for her. This provision, however, was a transitory one pending the next stage, when "Allah [would] ordain for them same (other) way." That other way was equal punishment for both males and females, as explained in the Qur'an (24:2), which is flogging (each of them) with one hundred stripes, provided that four witnesses testify unani-

mously that they saw everything in graphic detail. Such a requirement is practically impossible, indicating that the severity of the punishment is a statement on sexual morality in an Islamic society, and a deterrent from flagrant public indecency (see Al-Sabouni, M.A., *Safwat Al-Tafaseer* (in Arabic), Dar Al-Qur'an Al-Kareem, Beirut, Lebanon, 1980, vol. 1, p. 266). In the case of rape, however, only the rapist is to be punished, while the victim goes free. See A. Owdah, *Al-Thashree' Al-Jina'i Fi Al-Islam* (in Arabic), Dar Al-Kitab Al-Arabi, Beirut, Lebanon, n.d., vol. 2, p. 364; Ibn Anas, Maik, *Muatta' Al-Imam Malik* (in Arabic). Dar Al-Qalam, Beruit, Lebanon, 1st ed.., n.d., p. 245; and Sabiq, S., *Fiqh-us-Sunnah,* op. cit, vol. 2, pp. 427-428.

39   [24] *Sahih Al-Bukhari,* translated by M.M. Khan, op, cit, vol. 9, pp. 170-171.

39   [25] Al-Qasimi, Zafer, *Nizam Al-Hukm Fi Al-Shari'ah Wal-Tareekh* (in Arabic), Dar Anafa'is, Beirut, Lebanon, 1974, p. 342.

40   [26] Ibid., p. 342.

40   [27] Narrated by Abu-Dawood, also by Ibn Khuzaimah, who rated it as "sound" or "authentic." This is why some notable jurists, such as Al-Mozni, Abu Thawr, and Al-Tabari, are of the opinion that a woman may lead (both genders) in taraweeh prayers, (special prayers during the month of Ramadan), if no memorizer of the Qur'an

is present (see, Al-Shawkani, M., *Nayl Al-Awtar* (in Arabic), Dar Ajeel, Beirut, Lebanon 1973, vol. 3, pp. 201-202). Some of the Hanbali Jurists, following the lead of Ibn-Hanbal, agree with the same opinion. Ibn Taymiyah stated that "it is permissible for an illiterate man to be led in prayers by a woman who is reciter of the Qur'an in qiyam (prayers) in Ramadan, according to the more commonly known opinion of Ahmad (Ibn Hanbal)." See Ibn Taymiyah, *Ar-Radd 'Ala Maratib Al-Iimaa'* (in Arabic), Dar Al-Afaq Al-Jadeedah, Beirut, Lebanon, 1980, p. 208, quoted in Abu Shuqqah, A., *Tahrir Al-Mar'ah Al-Muslimah,* op. cit, vol. 3, pp. 31 and 60. The same opinion was reported by Ibn Qudamah in *Al-Mughni,* who added that it is permissible (for women) to lead men in taraweeh prayers and stand behind them. See Abu-Shuqqah, ibid., p. 31.

40   [28] Imam Al-Haramain Al-Jawayni states: "They [scholars] are unanimous that women should not be an imam [head of state], even though they differed about her being a judge in matters where her witness is accepted." The failure of Al-Farra' to include male gender as a required condition for leadership of the state indicates that the "unanimity" spoken of by Imam Al-Haramain and others is not such a complete "unanimity." Furthermore, Al-Tabari does not even limit the categories in which a women may act as a judge. See Al-Qasimi, op. cit, p. 342. Among contemporary scholars who are of the opinion that a woman may be appointed to any state position is M.I.

Darwazah, whose main argument can be summarized as follows:

1. The Qur'an provides for the **participation of women in the state, society, and all social and political activities**, except for few exceptions related to their gender particularity. Such allowed activities include parliamentary life and representation of all sectors of society; these activities include the participation in the making of laws and regulations, and the supervision of public affairs.

2. To oppose this on the grounds that Muslim women are "ignorant and unmindful" overlooks the fact that the great majority of men in Muslim countries are also "ignorant and unmindful." Yet this is **not a reason to deprive them of their political rights**.

3. Recognition of the political rights of women does not necessarily mean belittling or undermining their crucial functions as **homemakers** and mothers.

4. The fact that Muslim women did not participate widely in the political life of the community in the earlier times in Muslim history is explained by the **nature of social life at that time**. This does not in itself negate the rights enshrined in the Qur'an and Sunnah. See Al-Qasimi, ibid., pp. 342-343.

Bibliography

I. **The Qur'an and hadith**

1. Ali, Abdullah, Yusuf, trans. *The Holy Qur'an*, American Trust Publications, Indianapolis, 1977. Whenever necessary, slight modifications of this translation were made by the author of this work in the interest of improved clarity and accuracy.

2. Al-Bukhari, comp. *Matn Al-Bukhari*, Dar Ihya' Al-Kutub Al-'Arabiyyah, Cairo, Egypt. n.d.

3. Al-Bukahri, *Sahih Al-Bukhari*, trans. M. Khan, Maktabat Al-Riyadh Al-Hadeethah, Riyadh, Saudi Arabia, 1982.

4. Al-Nawawi, comp. *Riyad Al-Saliheen,* New Delhi, India, n.d.

5. Ibn Hanbal, Ahmad, comp. *Musnad Ahmad ibn Hanbal*, Dar Ihya' Al-Kutub Al-'Arabiyyah, Cairo, Egypt, 1950 and 1955.

6. Ibn Majah, comp. *Sunan Ibn Majah*, Dar Ihya' Al-kutub Al-Arabiyyah, Cairo Egypt, 1952.

7. *Silsilat Kunuz Al -Sunnah*: Al-Jami' Al-Sagheer, 1st ed., 1410 A.H. Computer software.

II. Other References

1. Abd al-Ati, H., *Family Structure in Islam*, American Trust Publications, Indianapolis, 1977.

2. Abu-Shuqqah, *Tahrir Al-Mar'ah Al-Muslimah Fi 'Asr Al-Risalah* (in Arabic), Dar Al-Qalam, Kuwait, 1990,1991,1994, vols. 1 to 6.

3. Afifi, M.S., *Al-Mar'ah Wahuququha Fi Al-Islam*, Maktabat Al-Nahdhah, Cairo, Egypt, 1988.

4. Al-Sabouni, M.A., *Safwat Al-Tafseer* (in Arabic), Dar Al-Qur'an Al-Kareem, Beirut,   Lebanon, 1980, vol. 1

5. Al-Qasimi, Zafar, Nizam, *Al-Hukm Fi Al-Shari'ah Wal-Tareekh* (Arabic), Dar Al-Nafa'is, Beirut, Lebanon, 1974.

6. Al-Shaw Kani, M., *Nayl Al-Awtar* (Arabic), Dar Al-Jeel, Beirut, Lebanon, 1973, vol. 3.

7. Badawi, Jamal, A., *Polygyny In Islamic Law*, American Trust Publications, Indianapolis, n.d.

8. Badawi, Jamal, A., *Islamic Teachings* (audio series), Islamic Information Foundation, Halifax, Canada, 1982, album 4.

9. Cheney, T.K. and Block, J. S., Ed., *Encyclopedia Biblica*, Macmillan, London, U.K., 1925, vol. 3.

10. *Encyclopedia Britannica*, The Encyclopedia Britannica, Inc., Chicago, Il., 1968, vol. 23.

11. *The Holy Bible*, Revised Standard Version, American Bible Society, NY, 1952.

12. Owdah, A., *Al-Tashrea' Al-Jina'i Fi Al-Islam* (Arabic), Dar Al-Kitab Al-Arabi, Beirut, Lebanon, n.d., vol. 2.

13. Sabiq, S., *Fiqh Al-Sunnah* (Arabic), Dar Al-Kitab Al-Arabi, Beirut, Lebanon, 1969.

14. Westermarck, E.A., *The History of Human Marriage*, Macmillan, London, U. K., vol. 3.